Eyes of the Sea

Vatsala Radhakeesoon

(Haiku/Short poems)

TRANSCENDENT ZERO PRESS
HOUSTON, TEXAS

Copyright © 2020, Vatsala Radhakeesoon

PUBLISHED BY TRANSCENDENT ZERO PRESS
www.transcendentzeropress.org

All rights reserved. No part or parts of this book may be reproduced in any format whether electronic or in print except as brief portions used in reviews, without the expressed written consent of Transcendent Zero Press, or of the author Vatsala Radhakeesoon.

ISBN-13: 978-1-946460-24-0

Printed in the United States of America

Transcendent Zero Press
16429 El Camino Real Apt. #7
Houston, TX 77062

Cover photo by Sergey Zhesterev
Cover design by Selwyn Rodda

FIRST EDITION

Eyes of the Sea

Vatsala Radhakeesoon

(Haiku/Short poems)

List of Publications

Whirl the Colours (Gibbon Moon Books, UK/Kenya, 2020)

Tropical Temporariness (Transcendent Zero Press, USA, 2019)

Unconditional thread (Alien Buddha Press, USA, 2019)

Guitar of Love (Real Vision Inc Publishing, UK, 2018)

Smile Little Butterfly (Alien Buddha Press, USA, 2018)

L'aurore de la Sagesse (French Poetry)(Scarlet Leaf Publishing House, Canada, 2018)

Hope (President's Funds for Creative Writing, Mauritius, 2018)

Depth of the River (Scarlet Leaf Publishing House, Canada, 2017)

When Solitude Speaks (Ministry of Arts and Culture, Mauritius, 2013)

Foreword

by Robin Wyatt Dunn

Vastsala Radhakeesoon is the calmest poet I know, and her poetry seems that way to me too: infinite still waters into which she drops her observations.

It must be the noir in me that relishes the moments when storms are threatening:

> Sky without blueness
> Howling wind flogs frail branches
> Paintbrush sings on grass

Yet even here the threat has a kind of delicacy: howling becomes singing. Because I am an American, with our tradition of 'Howl,' I hope to see more howling in future from Vatsala. But that is not this book.

Vatsala really makes poetry into a team sport, by which I mean she is a great friend for a poet to have: ever awake to the shifting gravities of this our absurd profession, and aware of—despite the necessary poverty and lack of apparent honors that come with this 'job'—the surprising number of attackers poets are likely to attract.

So this is Vatsala's storm too: carefully navigating the egos and ennuis of the peoples drawn to read and scribble poetry, for our thousand different reasons, yet all the same reason: because we find it necessary.

This book is necessary too: deceptively simple and calm, with a storm at its heart.

Author's Note

Haiku came in my life in January 2019 when I was battling against some unexpected ailments. In those depressive moments my mind, heart and soul felt the need for a break from the routine of free verse writing. I started reading micro- poems written by some of my poet friends online. Then I turned to the classics. I was soon mesmerized by the works of the Japanese Haiku master, Matsuo Basho and this motivated me to write my first Haiku book entitled *Tropical Temporariness*. *Tropical Temporariness* was published by Transcendent Zero Press in September 2019 and it consists of 42 Haiku about my native island, Mauritius. *Eyes of the Sea* is a sequel to *Tropical Temporariness*.

Mauritius is an island and thus it is surrounded by the sea. When I reflect about my native land poetically, I feel the sea is its eternal guardian/watchman. Therefore, the blue mystic sea seems to have a pair of huge hypnotic eyes that remain wide open on a 24-hour basis daily. This poetic association led to the title, *Eyes of the Sea*.

Eyes of the Sea comprises of 60 haiku written in the traditional style of 3 lines , 5-7-5 syllables. Most of the haiku in this book are about the natural beauty of Mauritius characterized by its tropical climate. I have also included some haiku about my visit to Orlando, Florida in March 2001 when I was in my 20's. Orlando in springtime with its blue sky and palm trees has some similarities to Mauritius and this made me feel much at home.

Being basically a nature-lover and firm believer in God, *Eyes of the Sea* is my way to invite humankind to explore the perfect creation and artistry of the Divine. It can also be regarded as a means to remind human beings to enjoy and stay connected to the simplest things in life.

Vatsala Radhakeesoon

Acknowledgements

I'm grateful to God for sustaining my inspiration and giving me the strength to write daily.

I also thank my sister, Sharda and my brothers, Umesh and Comal for their continual support while I've been writing this book

1

Golden fire now smiles
Cold baked earth heats in oven
Angry breeze freezes

2

Sun sparkles on leaves
Photosynthesis cycles
Yet old rose withers

3

Sun warms the blue globe
Sea rejoices in suntan
Sad ozone now sighs

4

Sun of Orlando
kisses the blooming flowers
Grey homesick rain dies

5

Soft sun of springtime
Squirrels are madly in love
Winter wraps Dot Land

6

Sunrays of winter
Blanket for shivering earth
Weak leaf catches cold

7

Blue sky of island
Sky of American Dream
Oceans now embrace

8

Tropical blue sky
Song of summer and winter
Flowers miss soft spring

9

Blue sky sings sunrays
Island pours tropical heat
Red rose wears raindrops

10

Humid earth shivers
Cats consult the Tulsi tree
Sunny sky sends hugs

11

A sky full of stars
hugs a madly in love moon
Light exclaims "Beware!"

12

Sky without blueness
Howling wind flogs frail branches
Paintbrush sings on grass

13

Tropical winter –
The penguin has lost its way
The sun still warms plants

14

Cold morning breeze blows
Sad pink rose counts its heartbreaks
Yellow bee brings love

15

Tune of grey winter
Foreign cats nap on the beach
Where is the white snow?

16

Long nights of winter
Shiny stars sing nostalgia
Kittens are carefree

17

Silent wintry night
Mother cat hugs soft kittens
Stray dogs shed hot tears

18

Cold tropical tree
witnesses birth of a bird
Old cat must now die

19

The sky is clear blue
Red ripe lychees veil winter
Advent of summer

20

Abundance flows now
Fruits, flowers and insects smile
Call from a cyclone

21

Chains of awful thirst
African land drums summer
Cool rain brings relief

22

Goodbye wool of sheep
No more slaying for leather
Welcome new straw hats!

23

Birds of grey winter
bid goodbye to green island
Tropical birds chirp

24

Sand hugs golden sun
Sea prides of soothing blueness
History churns pain

25

North, south, east or west
Whispers of sea everywhere
Warm exotic land!

26

The soothing waves waltz
The golden beach meditates
Tall filao trees weep

27

Roars of sea echo
Mad tropical trees rebel
Lotus is stable

28

Sea mystifies night
Sea glorifies calm sunrise
Shells sing tragic hearts

29

Witness of freedom
Witness of mad slavery
Sea locks History

30

Birth of an island
Screams of fauna and flora
Sea is the watchman

31

Storm shakes gloomy waves
Tropical wind chants fury
Immortal love sings

32

First ray of the sun
falls in love with white cool clouds
Brushstrokes never die

33

Dawn circles temples
God blesses all the creatures
A sick sparrow sighs

34

Dark night dies in dreams
God spreads the colours of dawn
Island hums rebirth

35

Pain of scary night
blends with chaos of forest
Birds of dawn sing Hope

36

Pink tropical sky
enlightens sea and green fields
Hectic sky weakens

37

Rivers meditate
Waterfalls kill the grey past
Golden dawn now wins

38

A fragile red rose
kisses the foot of Mountain
Respect the saviour!

39

Unique thumb-summit
stands amidst the blue-green land
Nature exclaims "Like!"

40

Sweet songs of fairies
mesmerize a butterfly
Mountain unlocks tale

41

Lion on summit
watches over greenery
Battle roars the past

42

Mother of island
nurses exotic baby
Dot-land keeps growing

43

Black volcanic rocks
embrace the furious waves
Mermaid sings a song

44

Scorching sun pours fear
Tropical earth sweats labour
Sugarcane fields smile

45

Deserted island
befriends toil of greenery
History sheds tears

46

Eastern sky wakes up
Sugarcane fields breathe freely
Brown rocks veil rabbits

47

Demanding green fields
reveal bitter truth of sun
Sugarcane is sweet

48

Greenery loves sea
Mad cyclones shout at Nature
Sun restores calmness

49

Gentle breeze of dawn
blows amidst sugarcane fields
Grey clouds hug defeat

50

Tall coconut tree
greets the tropical blue sky
Goodbye heat and thirst

51

Red lychees on trees
Gardens enjoy starry night
Feast for clever bats

52

Song of pineapples
blesses the tropical fruits
A break from winter!

Huge flamboyant tree
welcomes the weary creatures
Hello Umbrella!

54

Tropical red rose
writes a deep song for blue sea
Colours shine on flags

55

Lovely pink pigeons
return to their habitats
Anxiety dies

56

Mews amidst gardens
Feline study of blue sky
Respect ginger cat!

57

Kestrels of island
sit pensively on tall tree
Birds still miss dodo

58

Little grey picpics
circle tropical blue sky
Trees protect their homes

59

Cute cunning lizard
camouflages on soft green leaves
Trees exclaim "Beware!"

60

Tropical pigeon
displays coppery feathers
Crow whispers "Classy"

Eyes of the Sea by Vatsala Radhakeesoon (Photo credits)

Haiku 1-3 : Sun– Image by Thomas Schneider , Pixabay

Haiku 7: Blue sky of Mauritius 1 – Image by Mr_D, Pixabay
Blue sky of Orlando – photo by Carl Scharwath

Haiku 11: Sky of stars and moon – Image by Public Domain Pictures, Pixabay

Haiku 19: Sky and lychee – Image by Rattakarn, Pixabay

Haiku 22 : Straw hat – Image by Gerhard Gellinger, Pixabay

Haiku 24: Sea and beach 1 – Photo by Rajiv Groochurn
Sea and beach 2 – Photo by Rajiv Groochurn

Haiku 29 : Le Morne – Image by Nici Keil, Pixabay

Haiku 32 : Sunrise or dawn 1 – Photo by Pravesh Reesaul
Sunrise or dawn 2 – Photo by Pravesh Reesaul

Haiku 41: Montagne Lion (Lion Mountain)1 – Photo by Gerard Peka
Monatagne Lion (Lion Mountain)2 – Photo by Gerard Peka

Haiku 42: Trois Mamelles –Photo by Gerard Peka

Haiku 44: Sugarcane fields – Photo by Rajiv Groochurn

Haiku 50: Tall coconut tree 1 – Photo by Rajiv Groochurn
Tall coconut tree 2 – Photo by Rajiv Groochurn

Haiku 53: Flamboyant tree – Photo by Rajiv Groochurn

Haiku 55 : Pink pigeon – Photo by Keshav Nauthoo

Haiku 56 : Ginger cat 1 – Photo by Pravesh Reesaul
Ginger cat 2 – Photo by Pravesh Reesaul

Haiku 59: Green lizard on leaf – Image by Patrick 66, Pixabay
Green lizard with red spots – Image by Waszi, Pixabay

Vatsala Radhakeesoon

Born in the exotic island, Mauritius on 17 October 1977, Vatsala Radhakeesoon is the author of 9 previous poetry books.

She started writing poems in English at the age of 14 and kept on expanding her poetic skills in other languages such as French, Mauritian Kreol and Hindi.
Vatsala Radhakeesoon is one of the representatives of Immagine and Poesia, an Italy based literary movement uniting artists and poets' works. She has been selected as one of the poets for Guido Gozzano Poetry contest, Italy in 2016, 2017, 2018 and 2019. Vatsala currently lives at Rose-Hill, Mauritius and is a literary translator, interviewer and artist.

www.ingramcontent.com/pod-product-compliance
Lightning Source LLC
Chambersburg PA
CBHW041809040426
42449CB00001B/21